CW01309825

Kefalonia:
A Poet's Island Journey

By Ross Lane

Kefalonia
A Poet's Island Journey

©2022 Ross Lane
Cover design and image designed by Jeremie Bowles

The Author asserts the moral right to be identified as the author of this work. All rights reserved. This book is protected under the copyright laws of the United Kingdom. Any reproduction or other unauthorised use of the material or artwork herein is prohibited without the express written permission of the Publisher.

No part of this book may be reproduced, stored in a retrieval system, or transmitted in any form or by any means, electronic, electrostatic, magnetic tape, mechanical, photocopying, recording or otherwise, without the written permission of the Publisher.

British Library Cataloguing in Publication Data.
A catalogue record for this book is available from the British Library.

Published in the United Kingdom by Amazon

Second Edition: 2023
Print ISBN: 9798856112688

For Wendy Lane
And the Island she loves so much…

Thank You Arthur Cole, Nigel C. Williams & Jeremie Bowles

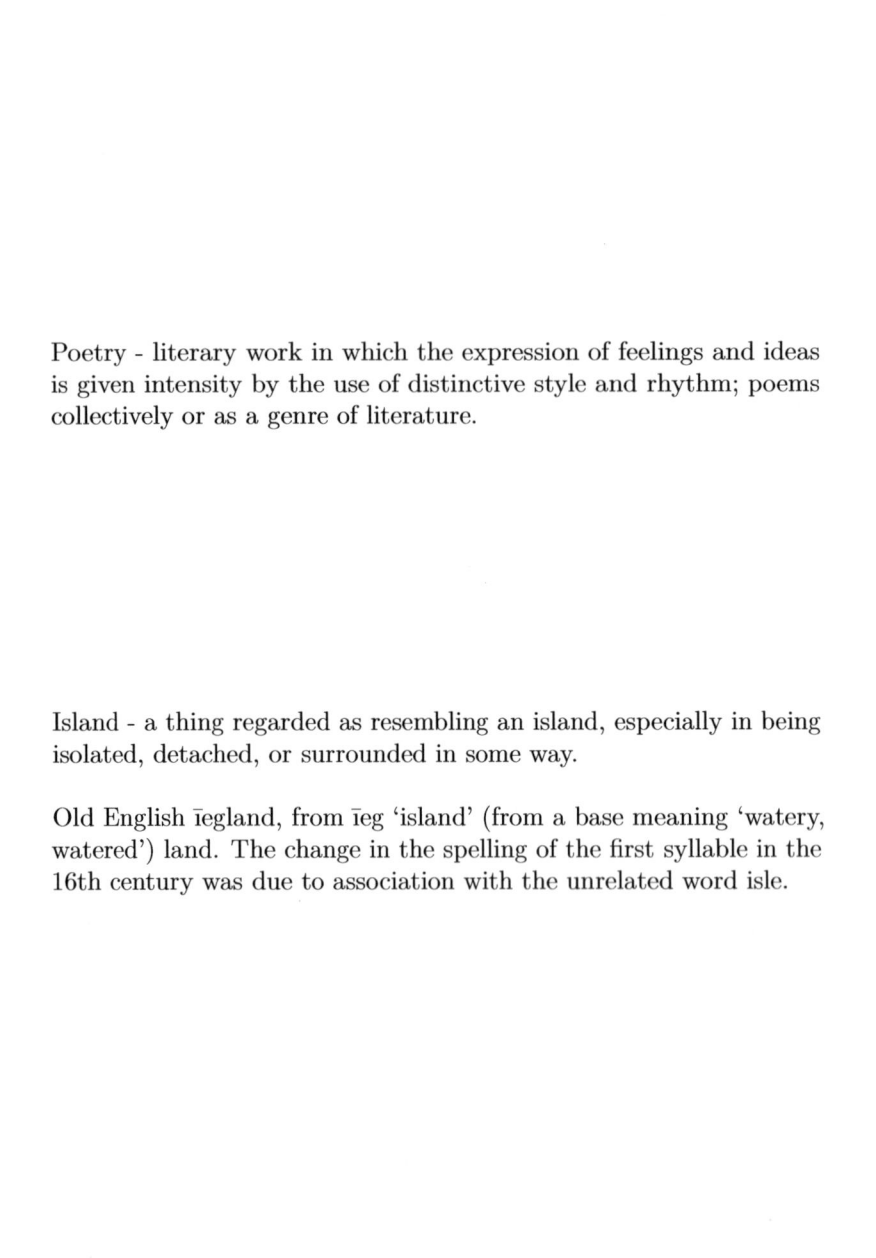

Poetry - literary work in which the expression of feelings and ideas is given intensity by the use of distinctive style and rhythm; poems collectively or as a genre of literature.

Island - a thing regarded as resembling an island, especially in being isolated, detached, or surrounded in some way.

Old English īegland, from īeg 'island' (from a base meaning 'watery, watered') land. The change in the spelling of the first syllable in the 16th century was due to association with the unrelated word isle.

CONTENTS

About the book	2
Foreword	3
About the Island	5
About the Author	7
Some Recommendations	9
Poetry Island	15
Homeric Sands	16
On Travel – A Proem	17
Cephalonia	18
On an Island	19
Assos	20
Memories in The Blue Hour	21
A Kefalonian Day	22
Myrtos Bay	23
Agia Efimia	24
A Place Outside of Time	25
The Fisherman at Sami	26
Farsa	28
Visitor	29
Lighthouse at Argostoli	30
Lourdas	31
Antisamos Bay	32
Bougainvillea	33
Natural You	34
Mythos at Sunset	35
Caretta Caretta	36
Odyssey	39
Maitre D'Hotel	40
Sunset over Lixouri	42
A Guide Book	43
From the Fortress at Assos	48
Gerasimus	49
Drogarati Caves	50
Skala	51
De Bosset Bridge	52
Mount Aenos	53

Contents

The Vines of The Hills	54
Where the Sea Could Never Leave	55
Katavothres	56
Ionian Sea	57
A Lazy Man's Approach	58
The Little House at Lassi	59
Island Sounds	60
Fiskardo	61
Agia Dynati	64
The View at Patrikata	65
Myrtos Beach	66
Melissani Lake	67
Kefallina	68
Going Back to Kefalonia	69
Pearl Moon	70
Kamina	71
Excerpts of Postcards from Kefalonia	72
The Goats with Golden Teeth	74
Earthquake Scars	75
In Sight of Ithaca	76
Lollygagging by The Sea	77
Beach and Back	78
Koroni	79
Light & Apposite	80
Epilogue for the Island – Part I	81
Epilogue for the Island – Part II	82
Epilogue for the Island – Part III	83
About The Book II	85
Making Memories	86
I Am the Island	87
Odyssey	88
Poetry Island II	89
Beach Walker	90
Discussions at the Peninsula	91
Lead Me Home	92
From The Edge of The Deep Green Sea	93
Excerpts of Postcards from Kefalonia	94
Poros	97
Kefalonian Moon	98
Fteri Beach	99
Steel Morning	100
Marooned	101
Tidewrack	102

Contents

Wine	103
Ocean Dreams	104
Memories	105
Dewpoint	106
Ocean & Adonis	107
The Journey	108
Tha Mou Leipseis	109
Echoes & Footprints	110
Thank You	111
Also by the Author	112
Anthology	115
Collection	117
Ensemble	121
Gathering	123
Fly Tipping	125
Driftwood	127
Highlands I - Proem	129
Beacons I	131
Ideologue	133
Journeyman I	135
Some Quotes & Reviews:	136

"I shall be never waterproof,
So please read me by the sea..."

About the book

What is it about an island?

There is a calling to these mysteries in the sea that captivate us, hold our imaginations and shape our dreams at every opportunity. This is certainly true of Kefalonia. Or is it a desire to be part of something greater, to experience a journey and landscapes worthy of Antiquity?

I have visited this island many times, walked its hills, driven its challenging roads and swum for hours in its perfect crystal seas. It is an island of pure beauty with dramatic cliffs, stunning pastel towns and sights so unique you can't really help but put pen to paper.

I have always been a writer of the moment and one who is truly inspired by scenery. So, each time I've journeyed around this Ionian island I have been quick to rush to the page and write down as best I can the stunning things I've seen. Kefalonia has a rich and varied history, it was the centre of the Byzantine theme, existed under Venetian rule, and was the sight of violent occupation during World War II. The great earthquakes of 1953 devastated much of the island and its scars remain today in the shadows of rebuilt towns.

In this collection, I have gathered some of my writing on the island of Kefalonia. It is a mix of old and new works that remind me of some perfect days beneath the Greek sunshine and a place I long to see again.

So, until I can rest my head again at the Hotel Mediterranee on this quiet, relaxing island, I turn to words I've written and dream once more across the Ionian Sea.

I hope you enjoy it. Thank you,

Ross Lane B.A. Hons

Foreword

I met Ross a few years ago, and ever since we have become very good friends, the main reason being that we are both passionate about all forms of poetry.

We are two totally different writers, with our own styles. I have been described as an "authentic" poet, a writer of times and experiences, whereas Ross is an artistic and emotional poet with a remarkable imagination.

Ross is a prolific writer, having already published ten incredibly powerful books of poetry. I would describe him as both creative and unique. His poetry takes you on a journey that opens up the mind, and creates an everlasting picture of the subject matter he writes about, whether it be a landscape or an historical event, for example I recall the poem 'Culloden' from his book 'Highlands' as a prime example.

Ross has no set template for writing his poetry, if a thought or an image comes into his head and inspires him, he has to put pen to paper and shape that thought, it's as simple as that for him.

He will then use that thought to sculpture and craft remarkable bodies of poetic work.

Ross loves to travel, and whether it be to the Highlands of Scotland, Australia, New York City or the Greek Isles, he somehow manages to capture unique moments, and transcribe them into an art form.

Once you have read one of his poems, you can just sit back, close your eyes, and I guarantee you will be there in the moment, that's how good his perception is of the subject matter.

I know for a fact that his frequent visits to the Greek Island of 'Kefalonia' have inspired him greatly, and he feels at one with her beautiful scenery, whether it be walking among the hills, through the small colorful villages or swimming in the crystal blue sea.

Ross's poetry paints a picture, and draws you in from the very first line e.g., 'Born of Poseidon's heart and nestled in Ionian wash' the first line from his poem 'Cephalonia.'

The line immediately gives you an image of the Greek God, rising up from the sea. I suppose you could say that Ross's poetry themes are about his journey in life, and his ultimate search for meaning.

As a writer, Ross sees the beauty in both light and darkness, and Kefalonia is the perfect metaphor for his poetry, as it's a beautiful island that has been scarred by multiple earthquakes over time leaving lasting effects. The collision of these two tones would speak directly to his writing shades and style.

If you read, or have read any of Ross's previous publications, you will identify that the search for self and meaning are key themes running through them all.

He has a style of his own, however on his own admission, there have been many individuals who have inspired him. These individuals are icons in their own right, Seamus Heaney, the Irish poet and playwright, Dylan Thomas the famous Welsh poet, David Lynch the film director and probably last but not least Mike Peters, singer/songwriter with the Welsh alternative rock band 'The Alarm.'

Ross by his own admission is a great admirer of all four among others, and has studied their works over many years. But if I had to label his writing style, then would class it as modern lyric poetry.

Ross and I have spent many hours discussing writing poetry, and how, at times, it can become a bit of a monster on your back and plays on your mind. Writing poetry can fill you with so many emotions, ranging from torment to delightful elation.

I guarantee that all the poems in 'Kefalonia' will hook you from the offset, and you will just want to keep reading about this beautiful island that has inspired the poet.

I would like to thank Ross for giving me the opportunity to write this short foreword, it has been a pleasure. I am sure that all the readers will thoroughly enjoy the book, and gain inspiration, especially if they are also putting pen to paper.

Arthur Cole

Author & Poet

About the Island

The island takes its name from an association with the mythical figure of Cephalus, who was rewarded for his war contributions with the island of Same, which later became known as Cephallenia.

There are also suggestions that the island is also the true Homeric Ithaca, the home of Odysseus, rather than the smaller island that owns that name in modern times.

Kefalonia, in the middle ages, was part of the Roman province of Achaea, but following losses to forces from the Western Mediterranean, it became a strategic location for the Byzantine Empire, blocking raids into the Adriatic and serving as a launching point for expeditions in Italy.

After the fall of Byzantine Italy in around 1071, the importance of the island was diminished, and the island suffered many sieges from the Italo-Normans in 1085 and later the Venetians in 1126. Kefalonia was captured during the Third Norman invasion in 1185 and became part of the Kingdom of Sicily until the defeat of its last Count and the island was conquered by the Ottoman Empire.

The island remained under Turkish rule until 1500 when it was captured by a Spanish-Venetian Army, and Kefalonia remained part of the Venetian Republic until its final days. The treaty that dismantled the Republic awarded the Ionian Islands to France who took control on the islands in 1797.

More war would follow. France conquered Venice in 1979 taking control of the islands and creating Ithaque, but within 1 year the Ionian Islands were taken again, this time by a Turkish/Russian fleet. Kefalonia was governed under the Septinsular Republic as a joint venture of the Ottoman Empire and Russia.

In the Tilsit Treaty of 1807, the Ionian Islands were ceded back to France who controlled them until 1809.

The British mounted blockades on the islands from 1809 as part of hostilities against Napoleon. After the Treaty of Paris in 1815, the area was recognised as the United States of the Ionian Islands and declared a British protectorate.

But resistance grew in the region and slowly gained in strength, not only to support the Greeks in the Turkish Revolution but also against the British. After several skirmishes with the British army, the focus became a Union with Greece.

Kefalonia became a full Greek State in 1864.

The island was dominated by the axis of power throughout World War 2. Initially it was the Italians but by late 1943 the German troops had become significantly present. The islands history is permanently marked by the events of the war and fighting eventually occurred between the Italian and German forces. After the siege of Argostoli, where the Italians held out, the German forces eventually prevailed and took full control of the island. There were thousands of executions during reprisals by the German forces and the island remained a state of conflict even after the war ended, due to the Greek Civil War.

Peace came to Kefalonia in 1949.

A series of earthquakes in 1953, where the Eurasian Plate meets the Aegean Plate created mass destruction on the island. The third of these quakes, with a magnitude of 6.8, was the most destructive, and had its epicenter directly south of the southern tip of Kefalonia, causing the entire island to be lifted by 60cms. You can see the effects today in the scars on the rocks around the coastline. The destruction was enormous, with only some areas in the north of the island escaping the damage.

In more recent times, the island has been a quitter place event wise. There were significant forest fires in the 1990s ruining massive square miles of forest, another earthquake on 2003 (5.3 on the Richter Scale) which caused minor damage, and another quake in 2005.

The island faced a major snowstorm in January 2006 where the island was completed blanketed, and then another forest fire in July 2007 when a major heat wave hit the island.

In 2014, an earthquake measuring 5.9 left several injured and properties damaged.

This overview is in no way intended to be definitive, but just to give you a taste of the rich history of this amazing island.

Notes:

Country: Greece

Region: Ionian Islands

Municipality: Kefalonia

Capital: Argostolian

Population: 10,633

Website: www.argostoli.gr

Coordinates: 38°10'24"N 20°29'27"E

About the Author

Ross Lane is the author of 10 modern poetry publications all of which deal with a search for meaning, identity and the course of life.

His publications can be broken down into two trilogies with "The Gathering Trilogy" being formed from his first three collections "Anthology, Collection & Ensemble," and "The Thought Trilogy" being formed of "Fly-Tipping, Driftwood and Beacons."

Ideologue, his ninth collection, is a stand-alone publication and Journeyman, a tenth publication is being released in 2021.

He is also the author of "Highlands: A Poet's Journey in Scotland" which deals with 25 years of travel through the magnificent Highlands of Scotland along with "Gathering," an omnibus of the first three releases with a selection of brand-new writings...

He was born in Wales, in the Cynon Valley in 1975 and educated at Aberdare Boy's Comprehensive School. He later studied at the University of Glamorgan where he obtained a BA (Hons) in English Literature, History, Philosophy & Psychology, during which time he learned from some of the United Kingdom's leading poetry authors.

As an avid creative he has been involved in many performance types from orchestras, swing bands, rock ensembles, short film and movie production both from a writing and performance perspective.

He currently lives in Cardiff Bay, South Wales.

Ross Lane's work is also viewable on Facebook (@RossLanePoetry) and YouTube (Ross Lane Poetry) along with Podcasts recorded with other authors.

Available Now:

Anthology – Poems by My Several Selves

Collection – An Intentional Collection of Poetry

Ensemble – All the Parts Working Together

Fly-tipping – Dusting off Memories

Driftwood – Approaching Thoughts

Highlands – A Poets Journey in Scotland

Beacons – Path's Punctuation

Ideologue – Just A Collection of Poetry

Journeyman – Wonderful Ordinariness

Gathering – Anthology/Collection/Ensemble: Together as One

Web Pages:

Facebook: @RossLanePoetry

YouTube: Ross Lane Poetry

Twitter: @RossLane

Parler: RossLane75

Podcasts:

Authors: A Writers Podcast

A Poetry Podcast

Publications:

Books are available from Amazon and other on-line retailers

Some Recommendations

Things & Places to See:

1. Assos

A small and beautiful town founded under Venetian rule. It is situated on a little cove and is a perfect place for lunch. The town is picturesque and surrounded by a stunning bay.

2. Myrtos Beach

There is probably not many beaches as beautiful as this one in the world. Its waters are a breath-taking blue and the views from hilltop stopping points offer amazing photographic opportunities. The beach is a perfect white and one of the standout sights on the island.

3. Fiskardo

The most northern part of the island, with a stunning harbour filled with shops and restaurants. A great place to stop and watch the world go by. I have heard it referred to as the "Greek Venice" due to the abundance of yachts and panoramic views.

4. Melissani Cave

A definite must for anyone visiting the island. This underground cave is spectacular, and you can take a gondola trip across the crystal chilly waters. It is a unique sight on the island and one not to miss.

5. Drogarati Cave

Walk among the stalagmites and stalactites in the beautiful underground world. The entrance was unearthed during an earthquake and the cave is said to be 150 million years old. It is a very rare geological phenomenon and an amazing thing to see.

6. Argostoli (Caretta Caretta)

See the endangered Loggerhead Sea Turtles and the only species that takes shelter in Greece. The best chance to see them is in Argostoli Harbour in early mornings when the fishing boats come in. They are between 1-1.5 feet long and can be up to 65 years old.

Food & Drink to try:

1. Kefalonian Meat Pie
2. Robola Wine
3. Mythos Beer
4. Kefalonian Omlette
5. Kalogiria
6. Kefalonian Extra Virgin Olive Oil
7. Riganada
8. Kefalotyri
9. Aliada
10. Myzithra
11. Bakaliaropita (Cod Pie)
12. Kefalonian Feta
13. Horiatiki Salad
14. Tirokafteri Cheese
15. Kataifi
16. Baklava
17. Mavrodafne Wine
18. Muscat Wine
19. Pastitsada
20. Kefallonitiki Kreatopita

PS... Did I mention the meat pie...???

Some Driving Tips:

1. Always give way to the goats.
2. Road surfaces can be slippery, even if they don't strictly look it at times.
3. Roads are narrow and winding... be prepared.
4. Roundabout Rules: Priority is to the driver who enters the roundabout. Once you are in the roundabout you give priority away.
5. Be careful on those hills.

A Good Day Drive:

Beginning at Argostoli, drive north to Assos, stopping at the hilltop for a perfect view before heading down into the little town. (The castle walk is spectacular.)

Returning south, stop to take in the view at Mytros Beach (Maybe a swim) before heading east to Sami, via Agia Efimia.

Enjoy an hour at Sami, or take a boat over to Ithaca if feeling adventurous.

To return, take the west bound route towards Argostoli for sundowners and dinner.

Some Other Things to Do & See:

1. Boating & Scuba Diving
2. Historical Tours
3. Wine Tasting
4. Archaeology Tours
5. Ithaca
6. Filming Locations (Captain Corelli's Mandolin)
7. Petani Beach
8. Agios Gerasimos Monastery
9. Agios Georgios Castle
10. Skala Beach
11. Koroni Beach
12. Argostoli Archaeological Museum
13. Mount Ainos
14. The Ancient Acropolis
15. Monastery of Lagouvarda
16. Kamina Beach
17. De Bosset Bridge
18. Katavthres
19. Monastery of Kipoureon
20. Lighthouse of Saint Theodoroi
21. Cyclopean Walls of ancient Krani
22. Roman Villa at Skala
23. Fiscardo Nautical Museum
24. Lixouri's Iakovatios Library
25. Monastery of Agios Andreas

Kefalonia:

A Poet's Island Journey

Poetry Island

If I can write you
Then I hope they read you true,

Spacious in limitation,
Still, and
Somnambulant at your commas,

And ornate in word and trope and sense,
Basking in each phrase and tense.

On this page
I wish them find you craggy at the corners,

And surrounded lush
In bounding main,
Cupped, in sandy sipping lips,

And dressed for show
Where slow winds huff and go.

Homeric Sands

If these are those Homeric sands,
Then you will see
Your own steps washed to poetry,

And when the tides recall your tales,
They'll simply say
Of all you left and what you took away.

On Travel – A Proem

Where some may say
The journey
Beats out the destination,
This may well be true,

But more importantly I'd say,
Just make sure
You never bring back home
The person that you took with you.

Cephalonia

Born of Poseidon's heart
And nested in Ionian wash,
Your chalky hills
Dashed with vibrant jade

Cut through the cobalt nest,
The still teal a gentle and
Slow lapping
Seating for your forest dunes.

The hilltop homes,
Pastel faced and bleached,
Line your watching sides,
Skirting ranges wide

And rolling green,
The knitted fields of vines
And the rubble scars
Of the shaken arc.

Your sunken coves
Cropped from dusty mounds,
Hold peach and cream abodes
Wrapped and flicked

By the blue-green splash,
Its single sound
Fills the so still towns,
The white based sandy bays
And the harbour's ebbing pulse.

On an Island

It could be argued
That the land here,
Timid in size
Beneath the sky
And ocean grip,

Is reduced in stature,
But also
The perspective can shift itself
Depending
Where your feet rest.

Assos

Hidden from time,
Pine and cypress seated,
And scratched

In soft-hued homes,
Curved around
A bowl of lucid blue.

Flanked at North and South,
Purlicue inlets
Drawing colours from the trees

To rebirth in aqua,
Each side the breakwaters cap
Stretching to hills foot.

Within your pebbled lapped port
The small boats writhe,
Near homes nestling

On craggy hillside,
While your perfect cerulean sea
Laps against your chalk dock walls,

Its crystal shifting palms
Urging sun shards from the sky,
Forming shades of newest blues

That probe and lick
Adumbral leafy pebbled shores,
That bask in clarion sky,

In a place of whispered time,
Venetian wall capped
Around San Marco's shrine,

Hill-bound at causeways tip,
Looking down upon
The stirring town,

Where every sound is born
On a gentle wave,
Stealing silent minutes from abiding days.

Memories in The Blue Hour

(Paralia Mirtos)

For context or indulgence,
I walk to find the poem,

To clutch it in the breeze,
The perfect vowels

And consonants of the thing,
Living and breathing.

The memories here
As accurate

As the footsteps in the dry sand,
But now

In the blue hour
I find the landscapes of my parent's eyes,

My father the nesting ocean,
And my mother is the land.

A Kefalonian Day

I am cast now
In the shape of a poacher,
And here
Upon this wooden stoop
I will hold this view
As a memory,
Still as a jar,
Idle as a painting,

The sky as an old frame,
The land a label,
The ocean
As a bottled peacock tail,
To later
Weep in recollection
Each time I open it
And take a sip.

Myrtos Bay

It's a thumb print gorge,
From coast hill inland cap
To bluffs sea nursed side,
Poseidon's print
On Kefallina's chalky rib.

Its basin shines
Of blue-green marble plumes
Smeared on the ocean plate,
Fading and folding
To meet the distal white edge.

The water's milky blue sheen
Wrapped in turquoise,
Laps the pebbled shore,
The watery mineral dust winds
Forming the loops, whorls and arches
Of the drink's friction ridges.

I've never seen so many blues
As potted in your bay,
A manta's waiting maw
Chiselled at coastlines floor,
Ionian's bauble beach
Where cobbles melt water bound,
And their zest swirls
In the cerulean wash that purls you.

Agia Efimia

If a picture
Then your waters
Add a blur effect,

Around a lazy port
At the hill-drop.

At the base
The buildings roost,
Nesting boxes

With coral caps,
And walls
So pale and soft and delicate

They fail to mute
The sun's glare,

While the tide,
Soundtrack to the harbour
Whispers at the subtle winds

That pat your ears.

A Place Outside of Time
Hotel Mediterranee, Lassi, Kefalonia

My delicious, tranquil, jewel sponge roost,
On Ionian shores in emerald burrow,
Squarish and stretched out boxy
With gleaming blue-eyes and oyster bark,
Pushing your sky back to the sea.

Molten crystal waters wash your feet,
Their sapphire shades lap and curl
Like a cobalt paw reaching and
Pulling the sandy salty shores to launch
And feel the thawing hold of purest teal.

I am lollygagging on your sea's stoop view,
Reclined and resting in lifted time,
As you excerpt the tautness of mind and self,
Ball it in your halcyon opal sky, and
Drown it beneath your moonstone brining wrap.

The Fisherman at Sami

The ocean formed a harbour lake
A solder still pit in morning's haze
Hugged by rising headland arms.
Beneath the concrete, fluffy clouds

A patent sentinel with net
On a wicker basket throne for trawl,
Hurling his lace snare to Ithaca
From a tired seawall perch.

The sea was rippled
Like a tankard's innards,
A stannic captured fist in landing walls
Gently waving,

The only rise from passing porpoise
Lifting like the oily sweaty knuckles of the bay.
The old man, removes his shirt,
His bones like a skin hanger,

And pulls the net in,
His right arm, like a hungry eel
Snatching at the haul,
Plucking the ocean's scaly fruit

From his vaulting lattice web
Dashing lardy skulls on concrete wall
And adds them to his loot
Before he flies the screen once more,

To the matrass covered bay,
This one hardly getting a drink
Before he pulls the netting in.
I watched it arch in the flinty wind,

But failed to hear a splash,
The old man like a conductor,
Catching the colours of the ocean
From morning leaden skies.

ΑΓΓΕΛΙΚΗ Λ.Σ 126

Farsa

There is a cave at Farsa
That watches Ionian tides.

Its wide cod mouth
A closing eye,

And at the lid,
Lined black against the sun

For fashion,
Its rocky innards

Pour upon the shoreline.
The beach

Is a sloping vanilla tongue
Thirsting at the ocean,

Holding it back to half moon
And teasing darker blues

Out to greener shades.

Visitor

From across the sea
I am here by wind,
To succor beauty,

To warm my skin
In weeping sun
And claim your air my own,

Until then
In simplest bonding,
You draw the change from me,

And post me back,
As relatable
As money is to trees.

Lighthouse at Argostoli

Lighthouse or pantheon?
I can see you at the headland
With walls of dripping cream
That let through the faded sky
And hill bandana.

The waters here
Are shaded as wild garden,
And on the man-made crest
You are still as a buttered wine cork

In firm and columned grip,
Like a static spinning top.

Lourdas

I have seen a beach
For tavernas and mini marts,

Curved like shoehorn,
And pockmarked here and there

With candy topped sunshades,
Filed on sugar sand

And marching
To the sea.

Antisamos Bay

From the air
So still
As a glaring bird's eye,

But then
With feet in snowy sand,
Your waters fade

To morning sky-blue,
Stitched
In tiny shadows

And hemming
Sands
In stunning envy.

Bougainvillea

To the touch,
No sturdier
Than this page
That clings to words,

Paper island plants,
Vine blushers
Hooked
On pastel walls,

These perfect
Bursting
Sun eating bulbs
That line home frames

Like building scars,
Summer,
On the snow walls.
Grown

From stone
And their twisted,
Hazel
Blemished trunks.

Natural You

What is the cost of feeling?
To be in here,

With all our noise
So trampled far behind,

And feel the honest nature of it,
To stand alone

In peace
And meaning's selfhood

With just the echoes
Of your own,

Then that
Is bliss itself.

Mythos at Sunset

(Trentis' Bar, Lassi)

To watch Lixouri steal the tired sun
Is perfect as itself could be.

The sky tonight is a burst peach
Awaiting bedding,

And upon the table
The frozen glasses sweat

Pouring tears for the lost day,
Ripping frosting from their heavy mirrored rinds,

And preparing the legs
For a gentle evening's chilling.

For John Lane

Caretta Caretta
Argostoli, 16/09/2019

Your very name is a summoning,
A chant or phrase
Whispered at the pier top,
A beacon
Calling you up and out,
You, the tawny domed
And beaked charging fish seekers.

I watched you haven-lid break,
Blade-winged and graceful
Slicing though the morning soup bowl,
Unfolding scenes,
Like a watercolour brush blot
When the green just wasn't right
And dried in boldest flecking.

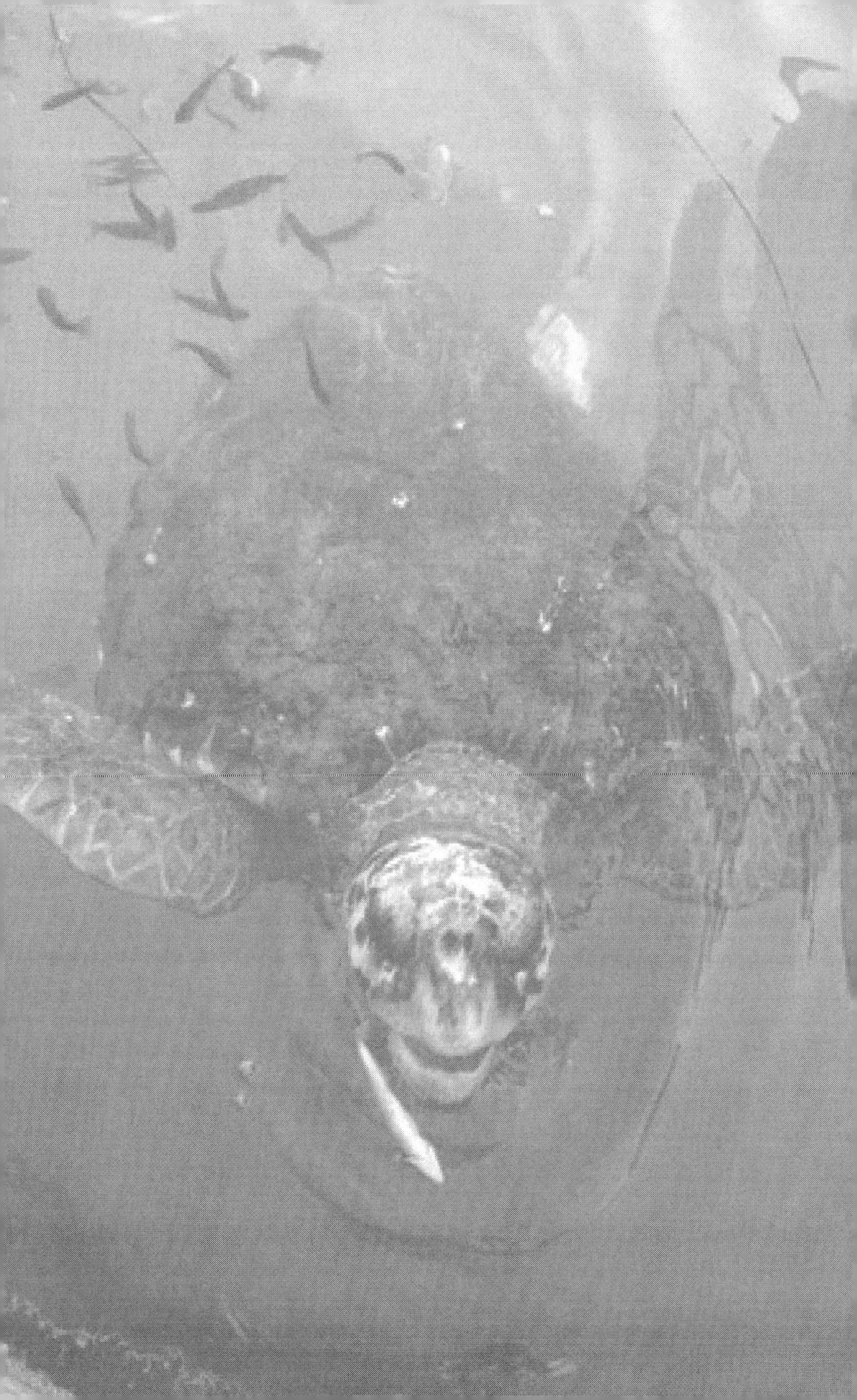

Odyssey

If I was never meant to find your shores,
Then why am I always found
Reflected in your sea's face?

Maitre D'Hotel

I have seen him
Take to a crowd like a maestro,
Directing,
Organising,
A marshal
For descending masses.

A courtly nod and smile,
Smooth as a tongue,
He places us at troughs
With waving hands
Like the paws
Of dreaming cats,

But suave
And assured,
A Greek "Arthur Fonzarelli"
Among a hungry throng,
And creating his legend
In traveller's myths and tales.

For Lambros Douvalis
Hotel Mediterranee, Kefalonia

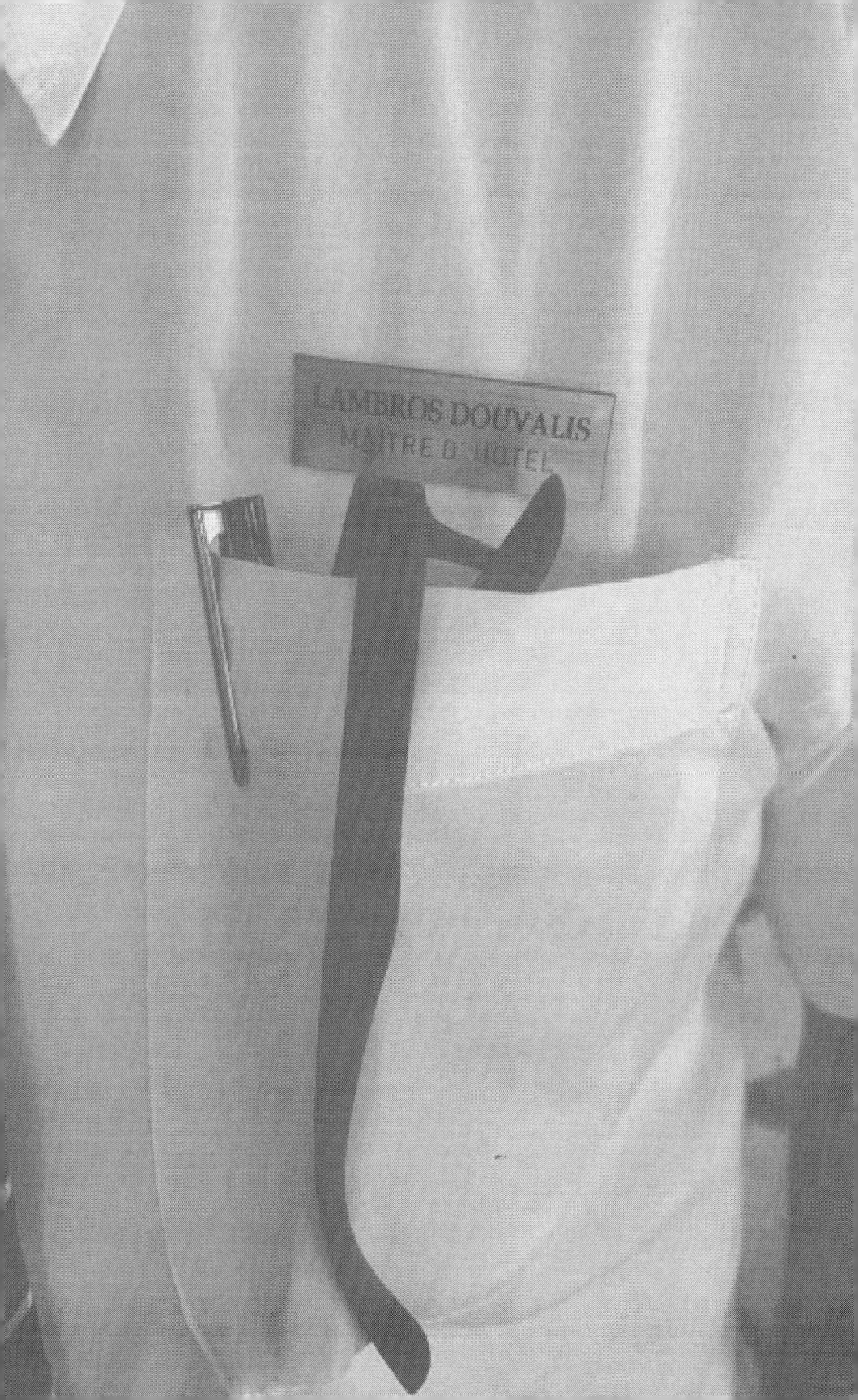

LAMBROS DOUVALIS
MAITRE D'HOTEL

Sunset over Lixouri

It burned it all,
The rocky shore burst
Like a pomegranate sliver,
And the Ionian wash
That loads this gorge
Is beaten plum and lilac,
Like Gerasimos' inebriant,
Pulped and fermenting
Beneath a coral-solder dripping sun,
And your smouldering crimson sky,
Burns at snaring heavens and
Melts to airy spring-songs
Fading
And washing over us.

A Guide Book

I have tried to shape some pictures,
Here
In scripted words
For paged theatre,

But my ink could never be
As blue,
And as your perfect,
As your sea view.

Lassi, September 2018

Journey -
A 'spell' or continued course of going or travelling, having its beginning and end in place or time, and thus viewed as a distinct whole; a march, ride, drive, or combination of these or other modes of progression to a certain more or less distant place, or extending over a certain distance or space of time; an excursion or expedition to some distance; a round of travel. Usually applied to land-travel, or travel mainly by land, in contradistinction to a voyage by sea.

Expedition -
A journey, voyage, or excursion made for some definite purpose.

Voyage -
A journey by sea or water from one place to another (usually to some distant place or country); a course or spell of sailing or navigation, spec. one in which a return is made to the starting-point; a cruise.

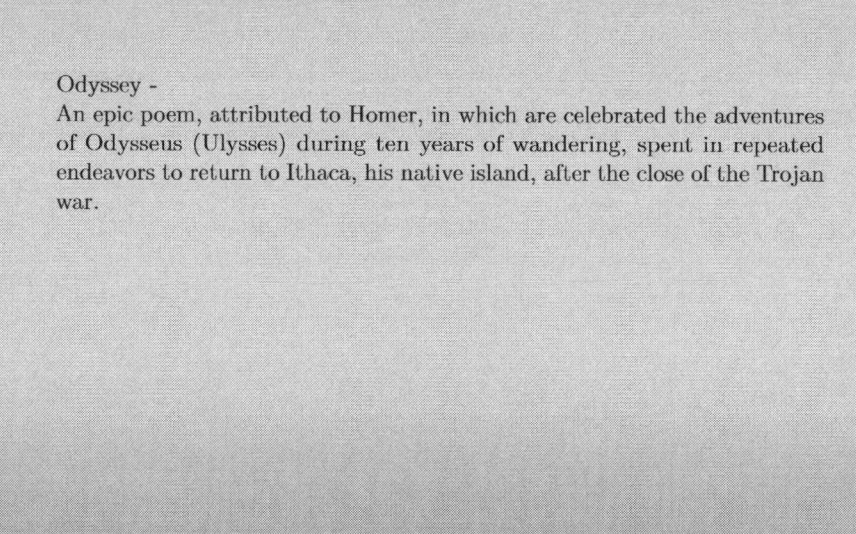

Odyssey -
An epic poem, attributed to Homer, in which are celebrated the adventures of Odysseus (Ulysses) during ten years of wandering, spent in repeated endeavors to return to Ithaca, his native island, after the close of the Trojan war.

From the Fortress at Assos

In gazing down,
Agia Kyriaki
Is still
As a morning smile.

The old walls behind
Are shaped from
Bubbled rocks,

In greys
And rusting thumb prints,
And here and there
They're slashed by weeds

But bricked
Ornate, and
Firm and true,
Around the gapping

Autumn mouth,
That teases down
The missing bell

That plugged
A sky frame.
And at the edge

Punched by bravest trees,
The cliffs
Are steep

And sudden,
Dropping off sharp
Like Robola on the tongue.

Gerasimus

As healing as the island,
They say each year
You float above the ill,
Passing over them
To cleanse their maladies,
Your frame intact
And death defying.
I loved the tale
Where you went door to door
In the aftershock,
Tending in comfort
To those
It caved within their homes,
Like a saintly beacon in the rubble.

Drogarati Caves

The island is blessed with amber pockets,
Laced with stalactites and stalagmites,
The optimists and the pessimists
Framed in toothy caves.

In exploration
The rock ushers to its balcony,
And on
To singing exaltation's chamber,

Where the residents of rock
In daylight, peel like slowing candles,
Making art of their very selves,
Where water drops click

And lick the rising and the falling,
While coloured column guides
Tease us to the still lake
So deep within your cloister.

Skala

There were pavements made of pallid chess boards
And lined in palms
Husk-dusted for dressing.

The town was huddled villas,
Jostling for the sea-view,
Woven tight on cobbled roads

And wearing scarves of fauna,
Taking the colours of the hillsides
To blot the building's whites,

But the beach was like a nursery rhyme,
Beauty to the eyes
And a beast below the feet.

De Bosset Bridge

Slung out in stone
Like lagoon's zip,
Straight and kicking left,
The toasted sandstone path
That heads to the other side,
Is hemmed in milk flanks
And bows
Halfway
At creator's celebration.

I thought it sought
To drift away,
But feel safer now in knowing,
The lights took root
To seabed's floor,
And though it seems
There's flexing still,
The land will not
Give up its crossing.

Mount Aenos

I saw you wake this morning,
Pulling quilted clouds
Across somnambulant brow,
While, at your hip,
The children stir
As day arrives.

Your arch
Is a whale back
With barnacle benches,
Placed for lollygaggers
Who tramp your forehead
Questing for the sun's touch.

The Vines of The Hills

There are shabby plants
In molten sun,

Like emerald fists
On sun-burned arms,

And lined on rocky, shingled isles.

There were grapes
As white as mistletoe

On plant centurias,
The guardians of the highlands

And the secrets of Robola's home.

Where the Sea Could Never Leave

I'll sleep
And bath in sunlight,
Where the sea could never leave,

I'll rest
And walk in moonlight,
Where the sea could never leave.

I'll wake
To roam in white light,
Where the sea could never leave,

I'll walk
On sandy lines by wet light,
Where the sea could never leave.

They'll say
The tides are timid,
That's why the sea could never leave,

I know
The enchanting truth of it,
That's why the sea will never leave.

Katavothres

Along Fanari road
There is a place
Where sea flows inland,
Bores itself
Through sandy rock,
And swims beneath
The island shins,
A river in reverse
Punching holes
That once ran mills,
Journeying,
To shine at Melissani,
Or short-cut its trip
To rest in Sami bay.

Ionian Sea

There's a shade to this water
That clings to this island,
And I have seen these blues
Before in gentle eyes,

Or I would show you in the skies,
If the clouds
Could nest and bob
Above the clear blue lid.

A Lazy Man's Approach

When I asked him
Why here?
He smiled
And waved away the stars...

Was it the silence?
The rolling sea,
Or leafy hills
That called him?

But in his eye
The truth bore out,
And he searched for himself
On an island,

Because of its beauty,
And
Smaller space
To look and search in.

The Little House at Lassi

There is a little house at Lassi,
Tucked away and hiding
Near a tiny little beach,
Where the sea crawls
And ebbs and flows
And hisses, gentle
As a wet eyelid.

But we could see ourselves there
In quiet hill-pocket,
In simpler times
With absent clocks,
Sitting on the loggia
Resting,
Looking,
And casting dreams into the sea.

Island Sounds

If you listen,
It's the wash
That grips you,

The perfect shush
Of ocean waves
That shimmer sand flats,

Lullabies
From sea floor shelves
That creep into the winds

To stroke your ears
In sunlight's warming,
And to the mind

A singing scallop chorus
Beneath the waves
Craving audience.

Fiskardo

Among the alabaster sails
The water swirls
In many greens,

And across your harbour
The artist has staged this town as palette,
Rested it a while upon the hills

And dared the waiting,
Perfect bay,
To steal the colours of his choosing.

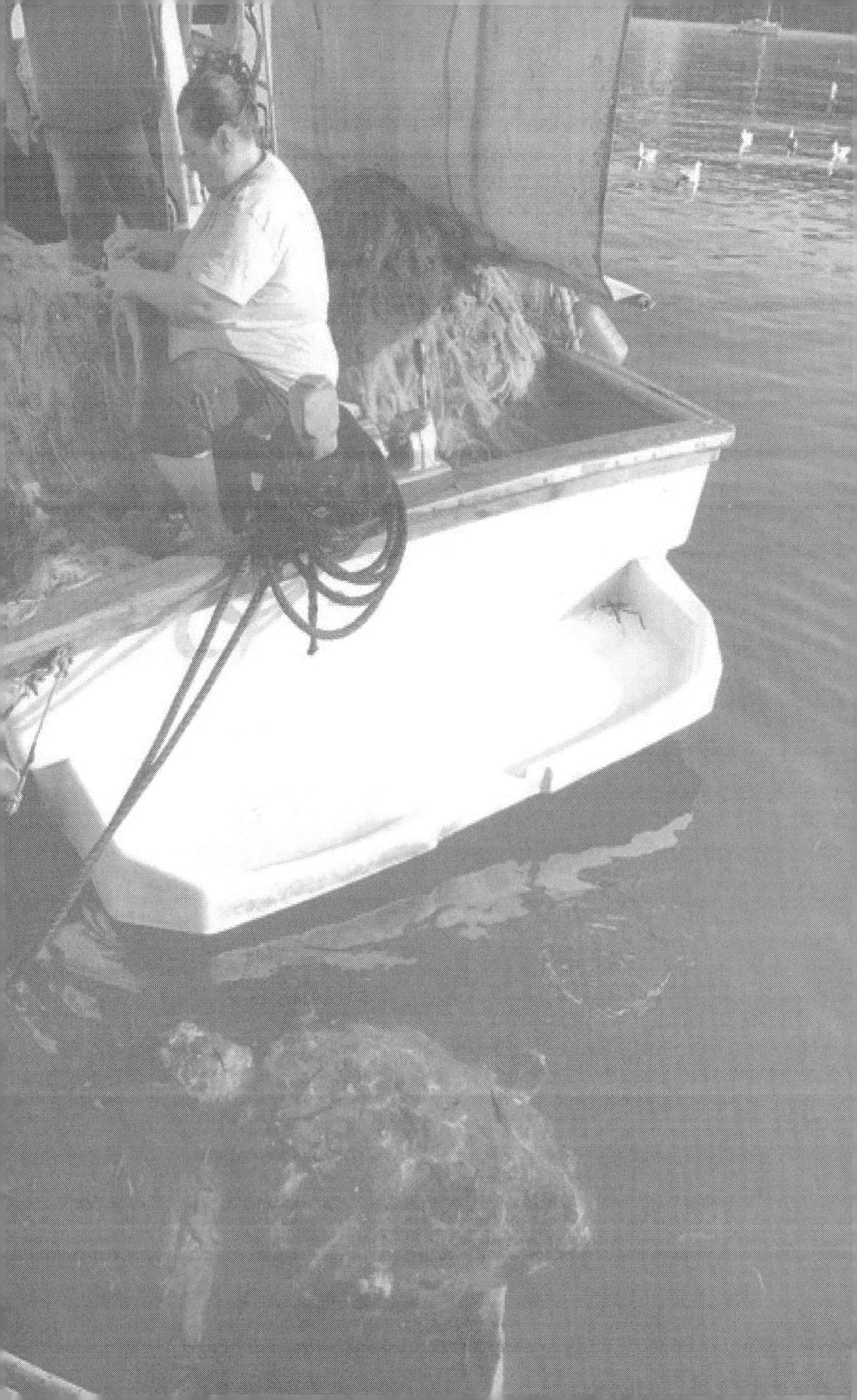

Agia Dynati

Above the tablelands of feta
Sleeps the meteor of Cronus,
Swaddled now
In yellow-greens,
Its face turned up to Zeus
And named
For absent saint.

The View at Patrikata

In the early haze
I can see the small town,
Resting on the flimsy lip,
That skinny
Pastel brace
That links
To emerald head,
The islands only claim
To the old Venetian crown.
And here
Your hillsides
Are as
Smooth as elephant hydes,
Bleaching in the sunlight
And drinking
From the painted sea.

Myrtos Beach

Most beautiful false prophet,
Perfection from a hilltop
A gorge
Of saffron wrapping gentle teal
In soft hush-wind and gossip.

At your face you're less sapid,
Your dove-mask cracks,
The whipping sand
Forms swarms of nettle-flecks,
And the sea is a siren

With pounding turquoise fists,
A grasper craving mortals,
Drawing all out
In joyful helplessness
Between undulant sapphire knucks and shakers.

Melissani Lake

It was an opal nymph pot,
An idyllic sunken world
Crater capped,
And rimmed with vine and herb,
Near the honey brown mouth
Of rock, cenote lakeside bound.

At shaft foot
The boatmen wait,
The singing gondoliers of the bowl,
Slapping charcoal oars
On rippled olive skin,
Ferrymen lost on pure azure
Beneath the still top socket
Of the vault.

The still pool glows
With fluorescent tears,
While smears of banked verdure
Splash its leafy coiling face,
A lakelet spring of turquoise bloom
Sunk beneath your dusty dune.

Kefallina

How beauty dark
There is
In earth scarred heart,

And you,
The bearer
Of this wound,

Shine today and always,
Haunted
In the basking sun,

Pulped alabaster
In the palm
Of turquoise

Deep
And shiny sea,
But fluff your forest greens

And soft-hued bricks
For all resting here
Like me to see.

Going Back to Kefalonia
(Paliostafida Beach)

The most seductive dreams
End with going back,
Ankles in the teal wash,
Bursting sandy grounds

To powder bulbs
With misty shoulders,
Shaping saffron clouds
On wading chalky feet.

The waves are lappers,
Breaking, as frothy seams
Along the beach arch,
And here and there

Sleep rocks among the blues,
Musician's thumbs
That score the waters,
Singing siren's song that call me back.

Pearl Moon

(From the Balcony at Hotel Mediterranee)

Tonight,
The Moon is a dropped pearl,
Cracked
And leaking,
On the silent, straggling sea.

Kamina

Beneath the hilly cape
There are nests
Within the sloping sand,

And hardbacks
Awaiting hatching,
Where the sea could never end.

Excerpts of Postcards from Kefalonia

I - Assos
At the hill base lay a small-town water splashed,
Nestled, silent,
And coloured flavoured-pastel-chalky
For perfect view.

II – Hotel Mediterranee (Lassi)
Standing there,
Time lifted like an old wet coat,
And my shoulders pushed up against the clouds.

III – Myrtos Beach (Pylaros)
Looking down
I saw its shades below the gorge,
A still azure marble gripped in perfect pallid pinch.

IV - Fiskardo
I walked the shaped and concrete harbour,
Gazing out at sunken turquoise lily pads
Stretched beneath the sea beyond the yacht-flock.

V - Sami
Wandering beneath the palm tree guards
You simply get to wonder,
Why the waves are landlocked
Near tabled-beryl-pond.

VI – Melissani Cave
In my memory we glided on the teal glass lake,
Deep within the old nymph pot
Under the channelled sun
That lights the blue sky's grave.

VII - Argostoli
The sun today rose like a cow's lick,
Waked the rocking harbour nested
And the hard-shells arrived to herd the old boats.

VIII – Mount Ainos

From here I can see to the edge of you,
Where your green ends and Ionian begins,
And out there rest the others.

IX – Antisamos Beach

I have seen your white sands break
From slope's green clutch,
And that thin band at your once cerulean breakers
Where the ocean mocks the hillsides dress.

X – Agia Efimia

The milky, blood-topped stores
Cast your boulevard grey under sun's slap,
And stir the ocean's shade to test it.

The Goats with Golden Teeth

On the hill crests
And mountain's shabby husks
You can see them posing in the daylight,
Shaded distinctly from the island's hide
And staring out to sea.

At first glance they may look like any other,
But then at times,
They show their flaxen smiles,
Blinding in the sunshine, bright and aureate
Like all who've fed from this land's loam.

Earthquake Scars

To reach the new town
We must pass through the old,

Those aged and sturdy frames,
Still now,
But blotched
In shaker's birthmarks,

Some held up
By vine armed trees,
Some hatless
In the baking sun,

But proud
Along the roadside,
Empty windows
With rusted metal galleries,

The sky within their mouths,
And their cheeks
So pale
With cracking pocks,

Like a walk through yesterday
To reach the now.

In Sight of Ithaca

There is a warming of the hands at the oar's top,
And a hiss at the hull
As I carve through the ashen lid.
But ahead
It changes

Sweating under
Lapis lazuli clouds
About the islands hem.

And now, with tired aching arms I push us onwards,
The boat elbows at the sea,
As I prepared myself for the crossing
And expected not the crossing
Prepare for me.

Lollygagging by The Sea

Between my toes
Paws the gentle sea,

Sand grasping
Like an infant,

So weak in hand
Or chewing maw,

That the sand
Evades her, mostly,

And the powdered slab
Beneath my rump,

Stays here as shingle plinth,
Or firm

As a sloppy bottle cap
That never frees time.

Beach and Back

Given the chance
He would tie the day
As a shoelace,

From here
To beach and back again,
Finding

In his still warm footprints,
The path
To places

Here and there,
The bliss of recognition
In each and every lap,

From poolside slumber,
To steps, to beach end,
To smile and back again.

Koroni

At evening
By the old tree,
The sand
Once white
Now dresses in
Saffron, flaxen shroud,

And the hugging
Emerald frames,
Darken
To meet the sea's drowsy
Languorous yawn.

They appear
Scratching on the shore,
The nesting
Shell topped waddlers,
With bulging eyes
And shields of nails,
Sandy egg backs
Shaking shingle.

Light & Apposite

Let all my footprints
Search
And aim for sand,
For there
They're perfect,
Resting
Whispy,

Beaded and changing,
Light in light
And apposite,
Sweet as memories
Lolled out
In recollection's low winds.

Epilogue for the Island – Part I

In a thought of perfect selfishness
I dream at least,
That though I leave
My beachy shabby footprints
Are never washed away,
Or taken by the sea.

Epilogue for the Island – Part II

From oldest days
The water showed the way,

Like the truth
Within the "Blue Mind,"

Or for youth's spring
Within the soul.

Epilogue for the Island – Part III

Nowhere before
Have I seen so many scars,
In sombre tales
Of Gods and man,
Of wars
And mighty nature,
Upon such a thing of beauty.

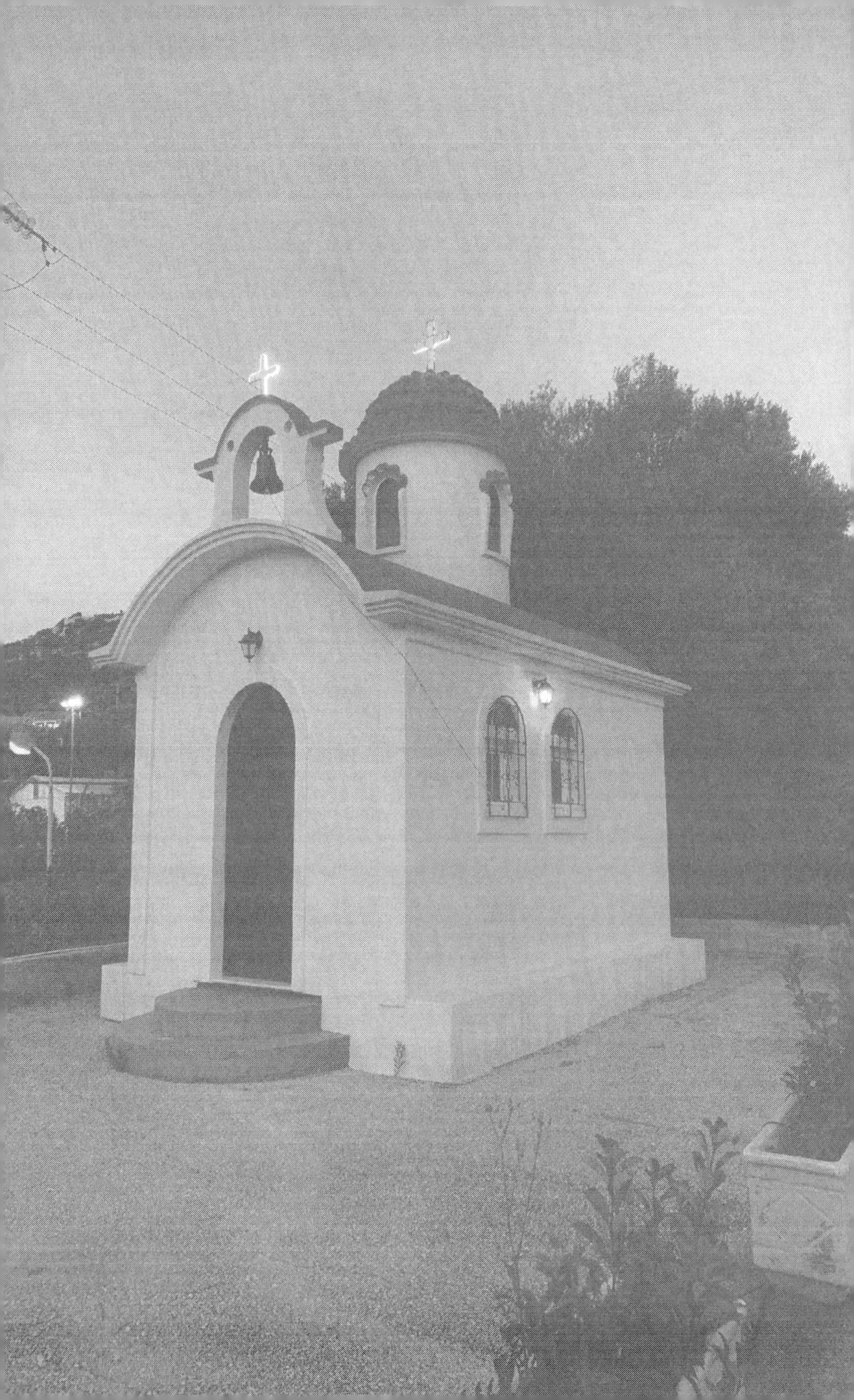

About The Book II

This book was a very different writing experience for me. My aim was to capture the rawness of poetry, that each piece should feel as new as its conception, a postcard thought captured in the moment.

I want the reader to feel the immediacy of poetry, to be within the breath of creation and understand my feelings when I walk this beautiful island. This is a place for navigators, and island beacon in the Ionian Sea and could never fail to make a writer write.

Kefalonia and its people are a subject very close to my heart (But you probably know this by now) and when this book was finished I realised that there was so much content that never made it into the first iteration, that the book itself wanted to evolve and grow, and it was this feeling along with yet another trip to the island that compelled me to write a little more, sort out the leftovers, and present this expanded version as a special edition.

So here's another 20 pieces I have written, something old, something new, something borrowed and something blue.

I hope you enjoy them,

Thanks,

Ross Lane

Making Memories

To shape them living
I look to the sea,
Deep and pulsing,
Ever-present,

And here
And always.

So, my memories
Shall be the sea,
And not the waves
With their shelf life of martyrs.

I Am the Island

My feet are washed in ocean wrapping,
And I am the island now.

Odyssey

I have shaped myself unbound
Wayfarer, scribbler
Adrift with intent,
My zest like a leaking Nautilus
Crying lanterns,

At times no more
Than a pain-wrangling sybarite
Bone bound,

But until then
At least
Contented,

Cheerful
Boundless
And shipwrecked on the moon.

Poetry Island II

Like a soul
The waves come at night here,
Shore lickers of assonance
That mop the sweaty brow,
Rustle at the beach grains
And shape the thing
For mornings viewing.

This itself
Is not unlike poetry,
You can wander through
The tranquil days,
Charge yourself with stillness,
And ready the page
For the waves at night.

Beach Walker

The sandy flat bed
Is a squeaker,
Dry and arid above the dribbling tide,

Who here
Is more loyal than the most,
Staying,
To whisper lullabies at blue hour.

My steps are shoddy,
And my toes' webspace
Each
The lips of a sandglass,
Catching and releasing

Throwing grains out here and there,
Time itself a flurry,
Until what remains
Is washed away.

Discussions at the Peninsula

After a breath
She said the sea here
Was coloured now as gin,
Clear and lucid
Under Hellenic sky.

And below its skin
The sun carved out some scales
Upon the drifting sand,
That powder bursts
On wallowed feet.

And when the clock ticked
She birthed the scene as poetry,
Pulled the island entire
Into her blissful heart
Balling memories in her chamber.

Lead Me Home

I will need no path
To lead me home,

Or degrade the old steps
That I have made,

But here I'll walk
On island sands,

Bare foot so skin
Can soak in land.

From The Edge of The Deep Green Sea

To dream
And beg the old moon
Cast me silver
On the slurring tide,

To be
In light and shadow now,
Where truth is out
And false still hides.

Excerpts of Postcards from Kefalonia

Volume II

I - Makris Gialos

A tropical cocktail
Sliced at mid-glass,
And rested still in jaded fist.

II – Saint Theodore Lighthouse

To see you true is special,
Rib pantheon of the headland,
A chalky cup poised for sipping sky.

III – Vouti

Sandy snare drum,
You rustle to the opal's wash,
A hissing beneath the wet toes
On chalky base with verdant cuff.

IV - Platia Ammos

Your steps crack like teeth,
And the only way
To feel the sea's kiss.

V - Petani

A slurred slough marble
Burst and trapped
Beneath the waves,
Where the land will not release it.

VI – Xi

The beach is a rind,
A coral apricot,
Or pumpkin husk,
The flame sheath for the ocean's blues.

VII - Agia Kyriaki

Beneath the sun,
Umbrella trees on whiten draw,
Freckles on the long beach
The tides never splash.

*

VIII – Platis Gialos

You are a pot of rocky oysters,
Resting,
Climbers who ache for shoreline,
And wait beneath the sea.

IX – Porto Atheras

There are lazy boats here,
Drowsy and somnolent,
And an old block of crayon
Shaley beneath the tree slide.

X – Avithos

Here the sand looks ripped from vines,
And at the beach cheek
The swarming sea
Churns the rusk to sabulous clouds.

XI – Limenia

Each step here breaks the silence,
I thwach and slap
And smack and snap
My feet on rock-ribbed flats.

XII - Agia Eleni

You are a pinch in waxy rock grip,
Among frosty bluffs that bake in sunshine,
Greening at the blue
And building echoes for the waves.

XIII - Lagadakia

Purple caps on wispy dunes,
You are soupy in the blue hour,
Lithic,
And warm and bashful as the sun fades.

XIV – Pessada

There are walls of cake
Near bottled beach,
A quiet rustle for the watching trees
And the water mimics back.

*

XV – Dafnoudi

Here is where the north pines march,
At halt above the cave mouth,
And the islands map is clear there
Sleeping in the sea.

XVI – Foki

I can see you through the olive trees,
The guardians of your bay,
There are pallid sands and grassy deeps,
And cameras to throw the sun back.

Poros

There is silence here,
The tides fail to mute
The craggy feet,

And at the road,
Palm trees grow as Grecian urns,
Sea gazing,
Stoic and swaying,
Husky and dazzling
In their form.

There are painted walls
Near laid back steps,
The ocean's shape
As blue on whitewash,

And above
The terracotta town
Is still,
Gazing out
At lifeguard rock.

Kefalonian Moon

The moon here is different,
Stiller in her smile,
Warmer in her soul,

She has loosed the world,
Missing now as clouds,
And birthed a new glow,

Highlights for the land,
Channels for the sea,
Master of her tides,

And everything else is lost behind,
The jewel all that's left
And we look up to drink her.

Fteri Beach

Show me myself in chalky window
As you have framed the sea,

Grasp me within the island rock
So I can always be.

Let me swim above the sunken stones,
The fingers drowned and still,

And I'll drift through skies of teal and saxe
In waters near the hill.

Steel Morning

The beach this morning
Is the lip of a paint tin,
Or an iron
Teasing solder
That rustles
Like the breathless.

You can watch the grey topped
Water flats,
Pawing and lapping,
The cheek brushing knuckle
Of Ionian's charm,
Present and coaxing.

Marooned

I am atoll-wrecked
No longer drifting,
The islet cracks
Through shiver swell,
Blue-green shawls
That hem fair bank,
A littoral cay
Cramped and narrow.

From this bitty key
On absent world
I have taken a powder,

Accepted Neptunian end
A failed and barren Orpheus,

Turning to the dust
I tread and walk on
That holds its fringe.

All that's here is me,
But at the inmost well's foot

The sky intrudes
To bring my soul to bay,

For I've lost touch,
Haunted by sense's driftwood

As the mists of evaporated selves

Whisper in the ocean's sighs.

I'll leave my breaking bones here,

On the flaxen dry
And pure shores
Of long-lost and cherished meaning.

Tidewrack

The sea abandoned it,
Sacrificed it on a tawny slab to Ra,
Scattered like so many tales
On arenaceous, branny shore.

They are the splinters of many,
The wanted and unwanted
Chunks and shards of other's lives,
Shredded, busted and dizzy from tides,
The shaded scraps of this and that
Dumbfounded on a sand bank
Waiting bounding mains reclaim.

The brine had shined them,
Washed off the wholly doubtful tints
From loose filed salt-worn pebbles,
This hogwash haunt of mishmash,
History cleansed in rolling swell
Seeking answers in a world of blue.

This deserted outcast plethora,
Once a precious or unsought cargo
In silent sob for former keepers,
But they lost them to the waves
And the ocean fly-tipped them on shingle.

Wine

Tonight the clouds
Are pockmark shells,
The wounds of rain unfallen.

The evening sky,
Russet and gold,
Crowns shadows
Webbing shorelines,
And still,
So silent still.

The sky is glugged
To hollow glass,
Succulent sweet and darkening,
Until raised
To tandem succour,
The mouth and nose,
The tannins of the land buds,
Elemental now, dark,
And slipping down the craw.

My glass is full of evening sky,
Helios' final hours
Swirl vinified here,

And set out present
To taste
And fully understand them.

For Alexandra Tzoumani

For bringing me wine...

Hotel Mediterranee, Lassi 12/09/2022

Ocean Dreams

I often dream to the ocean,
Its peace and shift,
The chill of its hold,
While I drift in every blue
The briny deep can brush.
At the surface I move
In its swelling pulse,
Smooth its face
With swaying hands
And walk its soft stirring base.
When I slowly wake
I leave my dreams there
To drift and writhe,
Dancing on aqueous gusts
Until shore cast in arid bands.
Standing on the shore I find lost dreams
On saffron banks,
Each grain once wonder, now
A fancy flaxen husk.

No longer fantasy or reverie,
They sprawl like resting fables,
Until your wet feet paste to them
And carry them away
To breathe and swim again,
Somnambulant scraps
Startled and circuitous.

Memories

Some memories
Can be lonely
And as want as an island.

At source,
Fuller than the real life,
Carefree and smiling,

Or heavy
As a yesterday
Depending how you swim them.

Dewpoint

We bottled boats at dewpoint,
When fore day crowned
Across stretching first blushed dunes,
The morrow's eyes still closed and gound,

Dream's debris crust on still sealed blinders.

We sculpted scenes at dewpoint
As the world burned in enmity,
The flame washed skyline of purest rouge

Framed our simplest scene while
Your voice blistered the air with gentle feathers.
We stole some hours at dewpoint,
The watch hand still at bubble's crown,

You brought the rain here
With gentle breath like ocean clouds,
And left me shadow chasing on frozen roads

Burning hurt in the embers of memory
And losing you to the whispers of the sea.
But if you'd stayed,
I would have washed you with my sandy words.

Ocean & Adonis

I.

It is all on perfect terms,
Cast me unbound
And drifting,
Yet, the pain I still hear,
Because as I swim
Your gentle assonance
Dies, rises
And screams between my fingers.

II.

The sea is an alluring badger,
And pulchritudinous
With the moon upon it.

III.

At that clock beat
When all of this is over,
You will find me on an island,
Out of this world
Dreaming again of swimming...
In a tale
I hope
Someone would tell and smile.

The Journey

Your map is cluttered,
Lined and contoured,
Washed with ocean
And shapes of land.

My compass
Was forged by generations,
Now rusted, pocket held
And searching.

I added the needle myself,
Floated on a shabby base plate,
Only my needle will do,
To search for my true.

Tha Mou Leipseis

This is where I hope we chance to part,
You,
Idyllic in dreamscape,
Me,
As empty as waiting,
But my words
Here are finished...
And I can miss you now.

Echoes & Footprints

I.

The sun is dark and cold here,
But I see your tranquil shapes
Forcing joy in tired eyes,

Who see you false in memory
And Flawed
As a photograph of water,

The flat feet ache
To warm on island ground,
And urge my soul to dream and dream

To coax my heart to sing,
To find me where your vines swing
To splash my ankles in your water's hissing
And wish for myself impossible things.

II.

So then
Until next time,
You're in my dreams
As the echoes of footprints.

Thank You

I don't think any poetry writer sets out to write a book... or maybe they do and I just haven't got to grips with that yet.

This book, Kefalonia, has grown from notes and etchings. It is a combination of years of writings, some at a computer, some on a beer-matt, and some on a pad that I keep near my bed for those thoughts at night that won't allow sleep until you scribe them.

If nothing else, this book is a love letter of sorts to an island that has brought myself and my family so much happiness over the years and is very dear to our hearts.

Thank you for taking the time to give it a read, and I hope it wets your appetite for poetry and other works I have penned.

Where better to find yourself than a quiet, gentle island?

Best regards,

Ross Lane BA (Hons)

Also by the Author

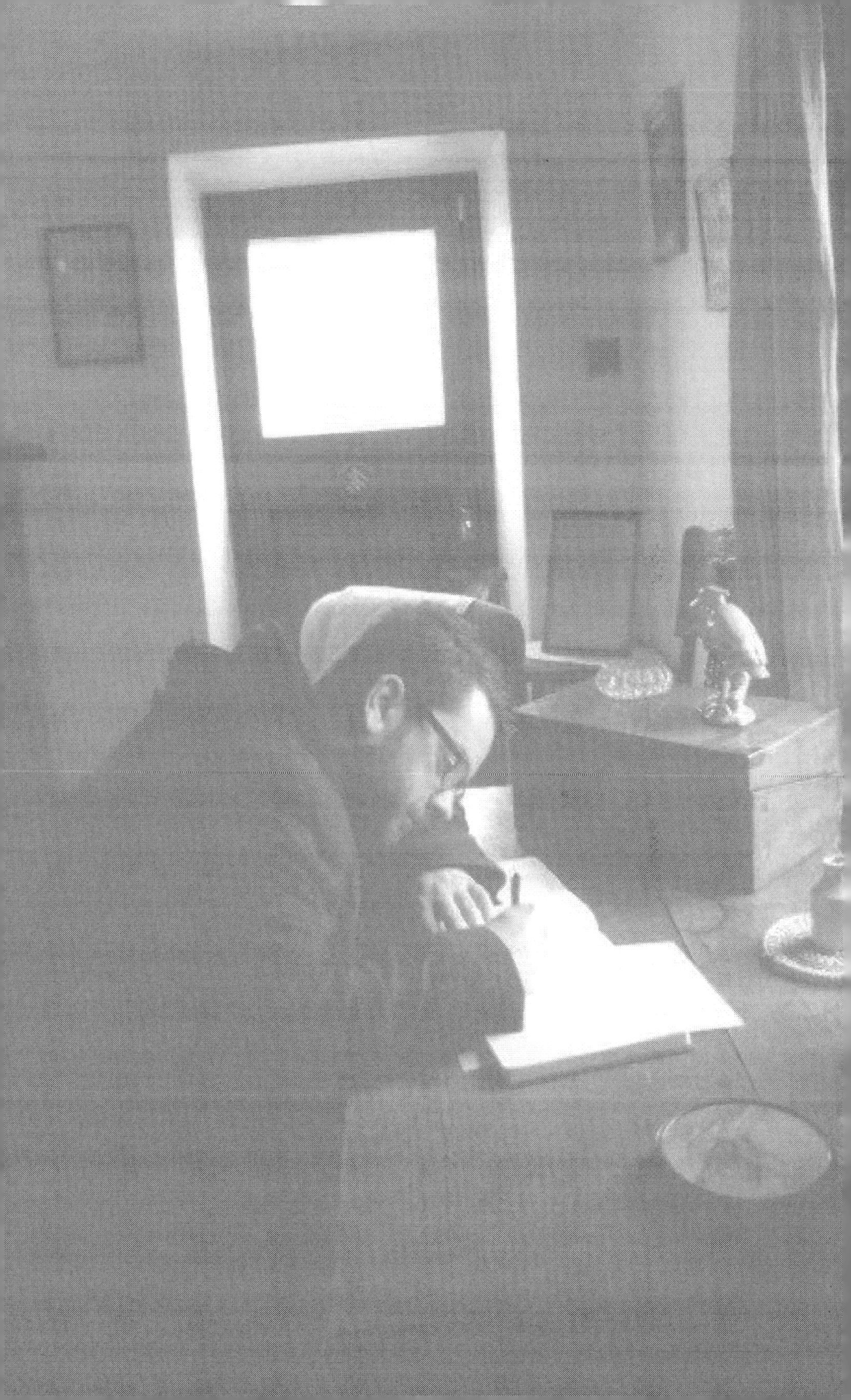

Anthology – Poems by My Several Selves

An anthology of poetry is traditionally a collected work by various writers and in a sense this is exactly what this book is. We are all different people at many junctions in our lives, we are molded and shaped by the people, places and events that leave their fingerprints and footprints on our souls, and as such we change and evolve, losing sometimes our perspective but at the same time gaining another.

This is a selection of work that spans 25 years of my life, the visions of my younger selves and the thoughts of a reflective poet looking backwards and forwards through the shards of all things that touch us.

Anthology

42 years of spectacle,
Memory's basket chock
With odds and ends,

Some return, some lost.

Fragmented illustrations
Of a then and now
Sometimes time and place,

Etched on fields of recorded light.

Memories form like an old photo album,
Different shapes and colours,
Tones of times and places
Different lenses, different faces,

The camera's evolved beside my perception,
Leaving plastic bound portraits
Of all the people I used to be.
All my selves clothed in gloss and matt collections.

My old eyes view
The joy in the documenters frame
And the smile of the child
And remember,

For once he was me and once I was him.

Collection – An Intentional Collection of Poetry

There is rarely an end to a collection, itself being the action or process of collecting someone or something into a place to be cherished, observed, reviewed and displayed. This is my first intentional collection of poetry, a selection of work that gathers further memories of people, places, events and dreams.

This book is about ownership, and the weight of responsibility we have to own our course when sailing even the wildest seas of ageing, it is the duty of responsibility to our younger hopeful selves who dreamed and willed us to deliver their future but have yet to face the challenges that life will deal us.

Collection

If you could see us now.
I stood by idle
When the fire was stolen
From your eyes,
When your wonder
Budding, new and naive
Was handed to strangers
Who maimed, mauled and
Crushed it
In the name of
Life and Love.

Did I fail you?
Each fall and turn,
When I bankrupt
Your catalyst,
Placing the precious
Pieces of your zest
In the hands of others,
Allowing their corruption,
Leaving a part of you behind
Each time.

So how would you see me?
Old, tired and jaded
Would you lay your future
In these aching, scared hands,
Entrust me
With the day ahead,
The hours that shape, the events that mould?
Would I earn the guardianship
Of eventual, forthcoming,
To lead you to the inevitable
And ensure your benefit?

It's not all bad
The view back from here.
You will see the world
And the world has seen you.
You have lost to love
And repeated,
And now with sleeve so torn
Your wear that heart
Upon your skin
Where no one could find it.
Barricaded from the mob.

Your brittleness now swapped out
Or wrapped in walls,
Secure and immune from air.
And the lost pieces,
Stolen or awarded,
Have been renewed,
Some ill fit the puzzles shape
Some adjust the visual,
But the core remains,
Harder to touch and see
But present.

At forty you'll run out of tears,
The soul's lakebed now dry and still,
Only gazing rearward
With pen or friend
To scour life's collection,
Just the parts that live in memory.

I sit across your shelf,
The mirror bookend of yourself,
And I judge my actions poorly,
Remembering that
I dulled and doused the burning embers,
Of the bright stinging eyes I see
In the long-gone yesterday's pictures,
Of the collection of our self.

But there's still a few sparks left
On the old blunt flint.

Ensemble – All the Parts Working Together

Through the writing of this collection I became fixated upon the concept of an ensemble, how it was all the parts of a thing taken together for consideration in relation only to the whole. This expanded my subject matter and areas of life that I wanted to explore.

I loved the concept that even the tiniest pieces of memory and life had a significant impact on who we are as a whole, who we have become and who we aspire to be.

It is a selection of poetry that gets away from the "headlines" of an individual and instead begins to peel back the layers that create the whole, the tones of our parts that create the orchestra of our souls.

Ensemble

Can you know each secret pocket?
Live surprise less with the entity of yourself.
Complexity laid out bare,
A transparent edifice
In crystalline frame,
The page complete without pens blood touch.

Have you gathered every bead,
Every stirring notion and thought that built the
Anthology and collection of owned ego?
Can you know all your pieces?
Have you taken each scrap
And sewn, or basted and tacked them to a whole?

Have you seen the true ensemble of your gift,
And the shadows it casts?

Gathering –
Anthology/Collection/Ensemble: Together as One

"Gathering" is Ross Lane's fourth publication and is an omnibus of his first trilogy (Anthology, Collection & Ensemble.) The collection brings the works into a single volume and offers a seamless journey through the books of self-discovery, reflection and understanding, with the addition of a selection of new writings only available within this volume.

Gathering

The caucus lay at the old tree stump,
Prodigal fronds on harvest's trek,
Equinox carmine blades adorned and splashed
Ash grey, bronze and chestnut chrome.

The mass had formed in glimmer mound,
A teeming dank and dewy shining drift,
Fall's meadow muffin the tree stub's gag
The tail end turret crowning above telluric orts.

Each stipule had gathered to form a rustic moat,
Around long dead stub with coffee lid,
A dithered tie around scaly mocha throat,
Autumn's decomposing hand in full wilt.

Each fallen bract shrinks in weathered crumble,
A mottled cape of oxblood red deforming,
Bleeding into each other's decaying frames,
Forming shades new, raw umber and lucid,
On the leaves of what we leave.

Fly-tipping – Dusting off Memories

"Fly-tipping" is the fourth poetry collection written by Ross Lane. It is a follow up to his poetry trilogy "Anthology, Collection & Ensemble." This collection is from a poet who has come to terms with the conception of self, its joys, limitations and agonies. It is also a collection from a poet who has become fixated upon time and its effects upon our lives. Ross' concept that poet's "Fly Tip" their memories through the process of catharsis comes across very strongly within the work, along with his thoughts and feelings around what the true impacts of time, then, now and to come, have upon us.

Ross refers to time as "the single omnipresent shadow of all life," a challenging force that we can either yield or stand firm against. In this collection he lays out his thoughts on this, the importance of having "meaning" in life and how the cyclical nature of emotional existence

Fly Tipping

I abandoned the inky logbook,
Time's channelled walls
I've bent and skewed,
The dust wrapper of matters
Can claim no lineage,
Each flap a jacket's wing
Beginning an end and
Ending a begin.

All prose forsaken
For recall's laments,
For dead-eye tales
Scratched on ragged pads,
Intermittent portholes
Lighting stern to bow
Or bow to stern and hull,
Dipping, teasing and jumbled.

These tousled thoughts
Dance a harrowing parade,
Aimlessly clutched
From memory's fog,
They exit, return and exit again,
Out of step, presenting a haggard case
Willing a measure
I will not draw.

I fly tip my shadows
So others might find them.

Driftwood – Approaching Thoughts

In this, Ross Lane's fifth collection of poetry, the poet explores the landscapes and impact of thoughts. The writer in this collection has likened the behaviour of thoughts as "Driftwood," objects that are truly free and moving, that never feel the impact of time, and come to us when both needed and unwanted.

In this book Ross looks closely at the value of thoughts, the productive and destructive, the valued and the haunting, and releases their timbre through a moving, wide ranging collection of lyric poetry that features works of place, family, love, memory and aspiration. The collection explores the raw nature of creativity, identity and relationships as the poet takes us away to the dreamscapes of ourselves and the malleable nature of our contemplation.

In this new book, the poet continues to ask the "hard questions" of the self, and explores the answers with honest, emotional and thoughtful outcomes.

Driftwood

My driftwood comes from Neverland,
And other elsewhere places.

Highlands – A Poets Journey in Scotland

Throughout his writing years, Ross Lane has been pre-occupied with the Scottish Highlands. It is a theme and a place that has surfaced time and again, a key cornerstone of the poet's palette.

This is a collection of selected poems from Ross's books where he has written about his many years travelling to the Highlands and the experiences and emotions that they have conjured in his writing. It is a place that is close to the poet's heart and a landscape muse, a scenery he is able to bring to life for his readers and take them to the very places he is describing.

This book also contains over 30 brand new works exclusive to this collection, that expand upon his themes, along with a short essay where the author candidly reveals why he is so drawn to the Highlands and reminisces about his first visit.

For Ross, the Scottish Highlands is an important presence in his personal and writing life, a landscape bold and intriguing that the poet finds impossible not to document, and generates enthusiastic lyric-poetry works about the times and places and memories it holds.

The book is a love letter to the beautiful Scottish Landscapes of the Highlands.

Highlands I - Proem

Most north and westerly well,
I will pull at rhyme in you

And draw diction from your mural,
Where leaning tawny hill flanks

Stretch themselves
From gaze to boundary's squint,

Like leaning, joining otters
Who kiss at sky's line.

And at your source
I am scooping at the spring

My hands cupped and still
As a fractured pail,

Panning out the unerring verb of you
On plain leaf.

Now,
To your eyes I do not know

If you'd call this poetry or not,
But I will paste you to my pages anyway

To prevent your ideal memory slipping
Like clutched water in my hands.

> For Barry, Penny, Jim & Matthew Aplin.
> Who have driven and loved those roads so much...

Beacons – Path's Punctuation

In this, Ross Lane's sixth poetry collection and follow up to "Fly-tipping" and "Driftwood", the poet expands of the themes of thought and life by shaping a collection built about life and its journeys.

This collection examines the poet's concept that whilst life is a free open expanse to navigate, there are "Beacons" along the path, destined moments of love, loss and challenge to be encountered in all our shared histories. Ross has likened them to mountain topping pyres that attract us, warn us and show our blazing trails through life's experience.

"Beacons" is a book about journeys, experiences and the joys or mortality. The poet takes us on an odyssey of sorts, highlighting times, places, people and thought, memory, aspiration and the impact of darkness and light.

Beacons I

I

Some are hidden behind wistful lure,
But they always emerge
Flaming, burning
And tearing open your dark sky.

Some are hinged
To reach out in path's punctuation,
Wearing masks
Of death or love to reach your meaning.

Others, the ambush predators of the trip
Will catch you then unready,
Refuse ignoring dormancy
And snipe at your heals as you pass them
Coda bound.

II

It's odd,
I can see them
Cardinal and scarlet tongued,
But
Still,
And mackerel blue at nub-jot.

Ideologue – Just A Collection of Poetry

In this, Ross Lane's ninth poetry publication, the poet examines the topic of thoughts and ideas, whilst evaluating their weight and consequence. The author has brought together a collection of writing that focuses on the creation, application and impact of ideas, and how easily their presence can influence the wider world.

Ideologue is a book about consciousness and wakefulness, and how, as a captor to some of our ideals, we can find ourselves forming conclusive concepts at the expense of embracing wider thoughts and notions. The poet takes us on a journey through the destructiveness and joyfulness of blind advocacy to ideas, and the ebb and flow of limitless or limited thought.

Ideologue

To the mind
It formed a verse of poetry,
Erroneous to some
False to others
And at times defective,
But he will clasp his meagre staff,
Shaped from bundled righteous kindling
And plaited around the axe head,
Charging and glowing and
So aloft
And swirling,
All will hear
The second-fiddled tune of it.

Journeyman – Wonderful Ordinariness

Journeyman is the 10th publication from writer Ross Lane. In this new collection the poet examines the connotations of life, its perspectives and its nuances. The poet has always been a writer who asks the toughest questions of the self, and in this new collection Ross once again sets out to understand what it means to be. The collection is a discussion on success,

beginnings and endings, and more. He has taken a philosophical knife to the concept of self-meaning and the social mirrors we hold ourselves accountable to. This poetry collection looks at the wonderfulness of

ordinariness. It is the search for beauty in the everyday, the sometimes beautiful and often mundane and macabre. The poet here is exploring the very kernel of aspiration, meaning and existence, finding both solace and challenge in the mystery of it. Is a journeyman a title to be sought after and held in revere, or a scathing damnation of a critique? Or is it all about perspective?

Journeyman I

Here,
Looking back upon the denary,
It all still has that "new-book" smell,
The fear
Is molten fresh and pulsing,
And you can smell it from the ledge
That holds
To show you my forever,
Rising from wells
To the very last of me.

What you read
Are just my songs,
Some travel-weary still,
But some, in ambition
Have flown high enough
To let me write the moon
To waking sleep.

At that working edge
I aim my pen,
With new shapes and old ones
Lost paths and own ones,
More assured now in outline
Chronotope and stem,
And through that path
Of hazard and wager know,
The surface here
Was already unsafe and scratched,

But do not worry,
I am quite wonderfully sad.

Some Quotes & Reviews:

"Ross Lane brings a lyrical intensity to the commonplaces of shared thought and language to crystallise the truth of things."
"Beautifully modulated. The personal and intimate seep into the consciousness."

Mark Jefferies
BA - MA

"I thought Ross Lane's Poetry was a great collection of thought-provoking imagery not immediately apparent on a first read. Returning to each several times you get to understand the depth of the thoughts behind the words."

Adrian Paul
Actor, Director & Producer

"Ross Lane's work never fails to inspire deep thought. He combines powerful imagery and beautiful language to capture the imagination of the reader and reveal his innermost feelings and thoughts."

Peter Wortley
BEng - MBA

"There is so much emotion in this stunning collection. Beautifully written by Ross and centred around the impact of time and the meaning of life."

Behnaz Akhgar
Television and Radio Broadcaster

"Ross Lane is a poet who captivates readers with his descriptive writing, and absorbing representations of landscapes, thoughts and memories. He creates a world of solitude and peace. These bodies of work are a pleasure to read."

Arthur Cole
Poet & Author

Journey's End... for now...

Printed in Great Britain
by Amazon

0f648c75-0b13-4cfc-bb54-9b95d816bd51R01